Miracle mbata

HOW TO COPE WITH HEARTBREAK

WAYS TO DEAL WITH HEARTBREAK AFTER A BREAKUP/SEPARATION

Contents

    1.

    2.

    3.

    4.

    5.

    6.

    7.

    8.

9.

10.

11.

1

HOW TO COPE WITH HEARTBREAK.

WAYS TO DEAL WITH HEARTBREAK AFTER A BREAK UP OR SEPARATION.

BY   DR.   MIRA   M.

3

TABLE OF CONTENTS

CHAPTER ONE

5

INTRODUCTION

Shock is exceptionally incredible misery and profound torment, particularly after the finish of a relationship or cozy relationship.

Grievousness is a tragically normal piece of the human experience, and it super sucks. We've all been there, and most would agree we as a whole need to try not to encounter deplorability at any point down the road.

We feel heart broken when we lose a person or thing we cherished or needed definitely, similar to a close connection or a fellowship, a relative, a pet, or a task or opportunity that was vital to us.

Deplorability can cause a lot of pressure, particularly in the event that the misfortune is an unexpected one. This pressure can influence how we feel sincerely and genuinely, and may require weeks, months or even a long time to recuperate from.

While there's still a ton to find about how and why we experience love and catastrophe and the impact these have on our bodies, logical review has furnished us for certain signs about why disaster causes you to feel so refuse, and a few procedures to utilize on the off chance that you're feeling truly down.

Concentrates on show that your cerebrum enrolls the profound aggravation of grievousness similarly as actual agony, which is the reason you could feel like your deplorability is causing genuine actual hurt. The language we use to depict misfortune - "I feel like my heart's been torn out", "it was horrible", "like an insult" - all allude to the manner in which we partner actual agony with close to home torment.

Love can be habit-forming, similar to a medication, due to the chemicals our mind discharges when we become truly connected to a person or thing. Dopamine and oxytocin specifically are chemicals which cause us to feel much better and need to rehash ways of behaving, and are delivered at raised levels when we're infatuated.

Then, at that point, when catastrophe occurs, these chemical levels drop and are supplanted with the pressure chemical cortisol. Intended to help your body's instinctive reaction, a lot of cortisol throughout some stretch of time can add to nervousness, queasiness, skin break out and weight gain - that multitude of undesirable mental and actual side effects related with deplorability.

These might be shock, distress, misery, disruption and dread; a yearning for the cherished to return; a longing for the individual who we presently dread was 'the one' from the start, and all the more worryingly, the 'one to focus on'.

We experience restless, nosy and redundant considerations of the adored, who has set off this most difficult hardship to our whole self.

At the core, all things considered, is disarray, incredulity and destabilization.

Painful side effects of feeling alone may before long follow, alongside consistent crying, defenselessness, sleep deprivation, weight reduction, and a powerlessness to get a handle on the destruction.

We have no clue about how to recuperate the injury - or regardless of whether we need to

Melancholy is a typical piece of a separation, however there may likewise be forlornness, absence of confidence or certainty, and profound trouble. On the off chance that you're encountering disaster as the consequence of a separation, make an effort not to seclude yourself from loved ones, and hold conversing with everyone around you, be thoughtful to yourself and don't pass judgment on yourself cruelly for the manner in which your relationship went.

With misfortune come five phases of distress: refusal, outrage, bartering, discouragement, and acknowledgment.

Notwithstanding how the case might be, separations hurt. We frequently depict the spouting vibe of a separation as the "condition grieved" in light of the fact that, for sure, the heart is breaking (however not truly).

This is on the grounds that the aggravation is genuine, basically the cerebrum thinks it is. As per FMRI, investigations of shattered individuals have uncovered that tragedy actuates comparative systems in the mind to those enacted when we experience actual agony. In certain examinations, the close to home agony individuals experienced was evaluated as comparable to "almost terrible" actual torment. Among these, different impacts of shock incorporate; expanded pressure, decrease or expansion in weight, sensation of sadness, humility, wretchedness and, surprisingly, self-destructive contemplation. Heartbreaks can be a great deal to deal with in light of the fact that affection is a medication.

Being infatuated assists the mind with delivering feel-great synthetic compounds like Oxycontin, serotonin and dopamine - these synthetic substances cause sensations of bliss and joy. In any case, tragically, these synthetic substances are the manner by which our bodies reward us for associating with others, and these synthetics can be habit-forming. Simply envision how it feels to reassess it or, all things considered, ingest away medications from an addict; there will be withdrawal side effects; the equivalent goes for heartbreaks.

6

CHAPTER TWO

The following are useful ways you can deal with your psychological wellness during tragedy:

Recognize the separation. Disavowal may be simpler, however recognizing the separation occasion will intellectually set you up for the hurt to come.

PERMIT YOURSELF TO FEEL

You will have a roller coaster of feelings; don't stop up those lines. It will burst the lines, so the sentiments stream.

Cut correspondences with the ex; you could need conclusion; in any case, their choice to leave lets you know they have pursued a choice. Kindly take comfort in that and continue on.

Watch the negative considerations self-fault and censure would happen this is only a cordial update that you genuinely deserve love and being cherished right.

LOVE YOURSELF

This may be hard to do, however it is just in adoring yourself and chipping away at yourself that you can recuperate from this hurt.

Going through your most memorable separation sucks. At the point when you haven't encountered misfortune previously, the wreck of clashing feelings whirling around can be a shock — in addition to you're confronted with the undertaking of figuring out those sentiments generally all alone. Then there's likewise the basic truth that, as a general public, we will generally revere the possibility of a first love: we find secondary school darlings faint commendable, and romanticize the thought of getting things right on the absolute first attempt. Truly, however, separations happen constantly yet — while a bombed relationship is literally nothing to be embarrassed about — that doesn't make your absolute first separation any less precarious to explore.

However much we could wish there was some enchanted valuable insight that could end up being useful to us quickly recuperate and continue on after a separation, that is basically not true — in light of the fact that each relationship and each separation is extraordinary

YOU NEED TIME TO HEAL

The lamentable truth? Recuperating takes time, and you essentially can't get to a superior close to home state without going through the whole, some of the time extended, mending process.

Separations are difficult, yet don't quit any pretense of all that you are doing in your life since you feel like you're not adapting and your life is self-destructing. Get some much needed rest, offer yourself a reprieve and you will recover financially.

REGRET WILL SET IN SOMETIMES

Post-separation, it's totally common to go over every last detail of your relationship in your mind and miracle where and how you could have screwed up — yet a lot of this perspective isn't useful to you over the long haul, and will just objective you more torment.

Do whatever it takes not to fault yourself for the bombed relationship

Conceivably the most troublesome truth to swallow after you encounter your most memorable separation ? This separation, no doubt, will not be your last so make a move to figure out how to return quickly from a separation in a sound manner.

Separations are in no way enjoyable to go through, particularly the initial time around, yet truly they're simply a piece of life that everybody manages in their own specific manner. The best anyone can hope for at this point is to stay cheerful, gain from every relationship, and spotlight on turning into the best version of yourself, so you're blissful and satisfied regardless of what your relationship status is.

DEAL WITH YOURSELF

dealing with yourself amidst grievousness is vital. Check in with yourself Maybe it's a solid plate of mixed greens, perhaps it's a hot shower, perhaps it's a call with a companion.

Additionally, realize that sensations of dismissal and lessened self-esteem could set off undesirable reactions like over or under eating or substance misuse, which could prompt a burdensome twisting and low confidence. Work out, nourishment, spending time with companions and adored one, legitimate rest will help the mending system.

MAKE AND EVALUATE NEW SCHEDULES/INTERESTS

Let's assume you truly partake in the outside, however your ex didn't, so while you were together, you cut back on your end of the week climbing propensity. Now that you're single, allow yourself to reconnect with that interest and furthermore investigate new leisure activities.

Let's assume you truly partake in the outside, yet your ex didn't, so while you were together, you cut back on your end of the week climbing propensity. Now that you're single, allow yourself to reconnect with that interest and furthermore investigate new leisure activities.

ACCEPT THAT CLOSURE IS SOMETHING YOU MAY FIND ON YOUR OWN

Now and again you won't finally accept reality you really want from your ex, and you'll need to think that it is all alone. On the off chance that your previous accomplice couldn't make sense of the justification behind the separation, make your own sound story. Likewise, on the off chance that your separation triggers contemplation and sentiments about different misfortunes in your day to day existence and you're struggling with handling everything, certainly look for outside help.

BELIEVE THAT THE PAIN WON'T LAST FOREVER

Whatever amount of aggravation you're encountering, attempt to accept that it will be OK and have confidence that on some random day you could meet your unique somebody who's genuinely correct for you. At the point when you're in the main part of catastrophe, it tends to be difficult to envision that you might at any point feel in any case. Yet, time will in general recuperate all injuries.

STAY POSITIVE

the separation shouldn't spoil the entire relationship. As the agony dies down, consider the great you received in return, embrace the fervor of additional opportunities, and remind yourself how astonishing life can be once in a while. Just consistently stay positive even through the genuinely torment.

7

CHAPTER THREE

Love can show you a ton life. Yet, the best educator is that of catastrophe. You absolutely never completely understand what you have until you lose it and along these lines can't comprehend love until you've lost it. Disaster is life.

Heartbreak is very great sadness and emotional suffering, especially after the end of a love affair or close relationship.

Heartbreak is an unfortunately common part of the human experience, and it really, really sucks. We've all been there, and it's safe to say we all want to avoid experiencing heartbreak ever again.

We feel heart broken when we lose someone or something we loved or wanted very much, like a romantic relationship or a friendship, a family member, a pet, or a job or opportunity that was very important to us.

Heartbreak can cause a large amount of stress, especially if the loss is a sudden one. This stress can affect how we feel emotionally and physically, and may take weeks, months or even years to recover from.

While there's still a lot to discover about how and why we experience love and heartbreak and the effect these have on our bodies, scientific study has provided us with some clues about why heartbreak makes you feel so rubbish, and some strategies to use if you're feeling really down.

Studies show that your brain registers the emotional pain of heartbreak in the same way as physical pain, which is why you might feel like your heartbreak is causing actual physical hurt. The language we use to describe heartbreak – "I feel like my heart's been ripped out", "it was gut wrenching", "like a slap in the face" – all hint at the way we associate physical pain with emotional pain.

Love can be addictive, like a drug, because of the hormones our brain releases when we become really attached to someone or something. Dopamine and Oxycontin in particular are hormones which make us feel good and want to repeat behaviours, and are released at elevated levels when we're in love.

Then, when heartbreak happens, these hormone levels drop and are replaced with the stress hormone cortisol. Designed to support your body's fight-or-flight response, too much cortisol over a period of time can contribute to anxiety, nausea, acne and weight gain – all those unpleasant mental and physical symptoms associated with heartbreak.

These may be shock, desperation, despair, disorganization and fear; a longing for the beloved to return; a yearning for the person who we now fear was 'the one' all along, and more worryingly, the 'only one'.

We experience anxious, intrusive and repetitive thoughts of the beloved, who has triggered this most painful affliction to our mind, body and soul.

At the heart of it all is confusion, disbelief and destabilization.

Excruciating symptoms of feeling alone may soon follow, along with continuous crying, helplessness, insomnia, weight loss, and an inability to make sense of the wreckage.

We have no idea how to heal the wound – or even if we want to

Grief is a normal part of a breakup, but there may also be loneliness, lack of self-esteem or confidence, and emotional distress. If you're experiencing heartbreak as the result of a breakup, try not to isolate yourself from friends and family, and keep talking to those around you, be kind to yourself and don't judge yourself harshly for the way your relationship went.

With loss come five stages of grief: denial, anger, bargaining, depression, and acceptance.

However the case may be, breakups hurt. We often describe the gushing sensation of a breakup as the "state of being broken-hearted" because, indeed, the heart is breaking (though not physically).

This is because the pain is real, at least the brain thinks it is. According to FMRI, studies of heartbroken people have revealed that heartbreak activates similar mechanisms in the brain to those activated when we experience physical pain. In some studies, the emotional pain people experienced was rated as equivalent to "nearly unbearable" physical pain. Amongst these, other effects of heartbreak include; increased stress, reduction or increase in weight, feeling of hopelessness, self-deprecation, depression and even suicidal thoughts. Heartbreaks can be a lot to handle because love is a drug.

Being in love helps the brain release feel-good chemicals such as Oxycontin, serotonin and dopamine – these chemicals cause feelings of happiness and pleasure. But, unfortunately, these chemicals are how our bodies reward us for connecting with others, and these chemicals can be addictive. Just imagine how it feels to pull the plug on it or, instead, take away drugs from a junkie; there will be withdrawal symptoms; the same goes for heartbreaks.

Here are five helpful ways you can manage your mental health during heartbreak.

Acknowledge the breakup. Denial might be easier, but acknowledging the breakup event will mentally prepare you for the hurt to come.

Allow yourself to feel; you will have a rollercoaster of emotions; don't clog those pipes. It will burst the pipes, so just the feelings flow.

Cut communications with the ex; you might want closure; however, their decision to leave tells you they have made a decision. Please take solace in that and move on.

Watch the negative thoughts- self-blame and deprecation would occur- this is just a friendly reminder that you are worthy of love and being loved right.

Love yourself; this might be difficult to do, but it is only in loving yourself and working on yourself that you can heal from this hurt.

going through your first breakup *sucks*. When you haven't experienced heartbreak before, the mess of conflicting emotions swirling around can be a shock — plus you're faced with the task of sorting through those feelings all on your own. Then there's also the simple fact that, as a society, we tend to <u>idolize the idea of a first love</u>: we find high school sweethearts swoon-worthy, and romanticize the notion of getting things right on the very first try. In reality, though, breakups happen all the time yet — while a failed relationship is absolutely nothing to be ashamed of — that doesn't make your very first breakup any less tricky to navigate.

As much as we might wish there was some magical piece of wisdom that could help us immediately heal and move on after a breakup, that's simply not the case — because every relationship and every breakup is unique.

The unfortunate truth ? Healing takes time, and you simply can't get to a better emotional state without going through the entire, sometimes lengthy, healing process.

Breakups are painful, but don't give up everything you are doing in your life because you feel like you aren't coping and your life is falling apart. Take some time off, give yourself a break and you will get back on your feet.

Post-breakup, it's absolutely normal to go over every little detail of your relationship in your head and wonder where and how you might have messed up — but too much of this kind of thinking isn't helpful to you in the long run, and will only cause you more pain.

Try not to blame yourself for the failed relationship

Possibly the most difficult truth to swallow after you experience your first breakup? This breakup, in all likelihood, won't be your last so take this opportunity to learn how to bounce back from a breakup in a healthy way.

Breakups are never fun to go through, especially the first time around, but the truth is that they're just a part of life that everyone deals with in their own way. All you can do is keep your chin up, learn from each relationship, and focus on becoming your best self, so you're happy and fulfilled no matter what your relationship status happens to be.

taking care of yourself in the midst of heartbreak is key. Check in with yourself maybe it's a healthy salad, maybe it's a hot bath, maybe it's a phone call with a friend.

Also, know that feelings of rejection and diminished self-worth could trigger unhealthy responses like over or under eating or substance abuse, which could lead to a depressive spiral and low self esteem. Exercise, nutrition, hanging out with friends and loved one, proper sleep will help the healing process .

Say you really enjoy the outdoors, but your ex didn't, so while you were together, you cut back on your weekend hiking habit. Now that you're single, give yourself permission to reconnect with that interest and also explore new hobbies

Say you really enjoy the outdoors, but your ex didn't, so while you were together, you cut back on your weekend hiking habit. Now that you're single, give yourself permission to reconnect with that interest and also explore new hobbies

Accept that closure is something you may find on your own.

Sometimes you're not going to get the closure you need from your ex, and you'll have to find it on your own. If your former partner couldn't explain the reason for the breakup, create your own healthy narrative. Also, if your breakup triggers thoughts and feelings about other losses in your life and you're having a hard time processing it all, definitely seek outside help.

However much pain you're experiencing, try to believe that its going to be okay and have faith that on any given day you could meet your special someone who's truly right for you. in the thick of a heartbreak, it can be hard to imagine that you could ever feel otherwise. But time does tend to heal all wounds.

the breakup shouldn't taint the whole relationship. As the pain subsides, consider the good you got out of it, embrace the excitement of new possibilities, and remind yourself how amazing life can be sometimes. Just always stay positive even through the emotionally pain.

8

CHAPTER FOUR

9

HOW HEARTBREAK CAN CHANGE YOUR PERSONALITY

Love can teach you a whole lot about life. But the best teacher is that of heartbreak. You don't ever fully know what you have until you lose it and therefore can't understand love until you've lost it. Heartbreak is life's most effective teacher. Unfortunately, what it teaches us isn't always accurate. We learn what we choose to interpret.

There are, however, lessons that we should all take from falling into and out of love – lessons that are universal. If you learn these things from the ending of a loving relationship, then you should consider yourself to have made progress in your life.

You realize that in life you just don't always get what you want.

Love is the strongest, most intense wanting that a person can experience. When you love someone, you want him or her; you want that person more than you have wanted anything else in your life. You want to spend time with him or her. You want that person to become a part of you. When love goes awry, which it sadly often does, you are faced with a list of wants that are, for whatever reason, unattainable.

You either want him or her to keep loving you or wish you could keep loving. But you can't. You tried. You failed. And now you wish you didn't have to give up on it, but you know it can't work. No matter how hard you want things to work, things sometimes simply won't work.

Most People Will Put Themselves First.

Being with someone and spending your life together is wonderful, but only as long as both parties deem it so. When one of the two people begins to feel that he or she is losing out on something by dating someone, that person will give up on the relationship and move on. If this is true for love, then it is even true for every other relationship we have.

People will always look out for themselves first and foremost. Love is arguably the only thing that can convince a person to put someone else's needs before their own, but love doesn't always last. Someone may be caring for you today and then tomorrow decide never to speak to you again because he or she is no longer happy. If the person you love can change in such a manner, it's fair to assume that the rest will be even quicker to flip on you.

Love Isn't Always Love.

Well, it is, but it really isn't. Let me explain. You are likely to fall in love with someone and then to fall out of love with him or her, and then the funniest thing happens. You begin to question whether or not you ever loved that person in the first place. You believed you loved him or her, but if you don't anymore, then did you ever to begin with?

Most people confuse love for infatuation or obsession. People get overwhelmed by their emotions and get fooled into believing that they define their love for a person. They may have never really loved that person, only thought they did. Just the same, they may still love him or her and not understand that they do. Love has many different faces and is misunderstood frequently.

Life Always Has A Way Of Surprising You.

Heartbreak is always a surprise. Even when you get fair warning, it still comes on as a bit of a shock. When you fall in love, you hope so much that it will be forever that you actually begin to believe it will be. Unfortunately, it usually isn't. Most people don't end up with the first person they fall for and not simply because they were too young to settle down, but because their first love usually isn't the right love. Heartbreak is just one of many surprises life brings our way.

The World Is Only A Beautiful Place If We Choose To Believe It.

No matter how we see the world, it all changes when we fall in love. Once we're smitten, the whole world seems like a better, more beautiful place. Everything seems better, more pleasant and less bothersome. We're focused, consumed by thoughts of the person we love and have little room or time to think about much else. Not to mention, when you're consumed by love, you can't help but be happy.

The funny thing is how this all changes when we fall out of love and/or has our heart broken. Things quickly change for the worse. This only goes to show us that our world is as bright or as gloomy as we make it out to be.

Emotions Are Fickle And Unreliable.

Our emotions are our natural drugs. They are the reason people use drugs to begin with: to feel more. We enjoy getting lost in our emotions because they are clarifying. They give us one specific feeling – one way of looking at and experiencing our lives at the moment. They rid us of confusion, confirming our thoughts with clear emotions.

People like to dwell on their emotions because it makes them feel more alive. This is why so many people like drama in their lives: They get carried away by their emotions and feel more alive. Unfortunately, our emotions are our own concoction and don't necessarily have to coincide with the reality of things.

Love Can Bring Out The Worst In People.

The more emotional we get, the more confusing relationships can get. Love can be incredibly intense, testing us and pushing us to the edge. When things start to go south in our relationships, many of us will start to distance ourselves from our partner or even attack him or her directly because we blame our partner – even if only secretly – for our current distress.

Love isn't always clear and can often be confusing. When confused, many individuals go on the offensive and start to poke at his or her lover's weaknesses. I'm not exactly sure why this is, but I feel like we're trying to test our partners and see if we can push them to the point of breaking before we break. That way, we can blame the relationship falling apart on them, instead of taking responsibility ourselves.

Life Always Goes On.

Love brings us to the gates of heaven and then watches us as we crash back down to earth. But we usually survive the fall. More importantly, we all can survive the fall if we keep our head on straight and understand that all we are experiencing is a natural part of human life. Life will go on and we will keep living, long after we have our hearts broken the first time, second time or third time. No matter how bad our situation may seem, it will all one day be a distant memory.

Nothing In The World Is Entirely Self-Sustainable.

Being naïve, we think the perfect relationship with the right person will be easy and require little maintenance. We believe it should be so natural that it fits together seamlessly. Unfortunately, I have yet to come across anything in life, completely natural or otherwise, that doesn't require some effort to maintain.

That's why most relationships fail – the same reason most endeavors fail: People think they've won before they've won. You only win on the day you die, having lived and loved the way you wish you had. Everything up to that point is still part of the game. You're not done playing until you can't play any longer. Until then, you better put in the required effort or risk losing it all.

10

CHAPTER FIVE

SIGNS YOUR HEARTBREAK CHANGED YOU IN A GOOD WAY

1. You started being more calculated when you approach someone you like, you take it one step at a time and you make sure that both of you are on the same page before you jump to conclusions.

2. You've become more guarded but in a good way. It's not like you given up on love but you're just saving your heart for those who really want it instead of being reckless with it.

3. You don't ignore the red flags just because you really like someone. You either address them or walk away instead of making excuses or pretending that they don't bother you.

4. You stopped giving your <u>exes</u> the chance to come back into your life because you've already moved on and understood why they were not right for you.

5. You know that if someone likes you, you'll *feel* it and *know* it, you don't spend your time analyzing, questioning, guessing or wondering.

6. You don't date to fill a void anymore or because you feel lonely. You just try to distract yourself with other things until you find someone you genuinely like.

7. You're not afraid of getting heartbroken again. You know that it's a risk you're taking with every relationship you get in and you know that you're capable of moving on when things get too hard.

8. You don't fight for people who don't fight for you. You learn to let the ones who don't care go.

9. You don't believe in almost relationships anymore. You know that love shouldn't be an *almost* thing and that it only means that someone is not serious about you.

10. You know how to embrace the single life and enjoy doing the things that you can't really do once you're in a relationship.

11. You invest more in other important relationships in your life; like your family, your friends and your colleagues.

12. You've learned that infatuation doesn't keep a relationship going and it's only *temporary*. You look for deeper qualities that could last.

13. You get to know yourself better and this helps you understand specifically what you want in a partner so you make better decisions in the future.

14. You remain positive and hopeful about love, even after a few heart breaks because they're just stepping-stones leading you to find the right person and the right kind of love.

Break ups can really do a number on our perspective, they make our entire world look extremely dark and take away our positivity and faith for the future. That's why affirmations can be such a valuable tool in helping shift that perspective.

You can utilize the affirmations below in a couple different ways- traditionally they're said out loud so you can hear yourself saying them, but my favorite way is to write them down every morning in my journal. The key to this is consistency, I would also write them down on a post it note and stick it at my desk so I can see it all day. Take some time to figure out what works for you.

Last note: Some of these might not feel "genuine" to you, meaning you don't believe them yet. That's OK! That's another great way to use affirmations to help you "act as if" you believe these things until your heart catches up.

11

AFFIRMATIONS WHEN YOU ARE GOING THROUGH A BREAKUP

I trust that this will pass.

I did my best in my last relationship.

I know that one day I will see this as a blessing in disguise.

I accept my feelings as they are.

I accept this break up for what it is.

I know that I will be in the most beautiful relationship someday.

I am ok, I am safe.

I am loved, loving, and lovable.

Only I can determine my worth.

I have so much to be grateful for.

My heart will heal.

I am so deserving of a loving relationship.

I forgive myself.

I trust that I am taken care of.

I am allowing myself to let go.

I take care of myself.

I give myself permission to heal.

I am worthy of love.

I am enough.

I trust this is happening exactly as it should.

I am strong and powerful.

I   release   what   doesn't   serve   me.

12

SIGNS YOU HAVE MOVED ON FROM A BREAK UP

You've deleted all the photos and videos

For some people, this is the very first thing they do when being dumped. For others, this is the very last step. A lot of people keep photos, videos and texts on their phones or computers, telling themselves "Oh, it's just a photo". But the truth is, these are things that are holding you (subconsciously) from moving on. Deleting all these things means acceptance – that he or she is never calling you back and that you two are never getting back together.

You've stopped stalking your ex on social media

The more you keep yourself in touch with their lives, the harder it becomes for you to distance yourself from them. More so if they're in your friend list. How to know you've moved on? That's when you have removed her or him completely from your digital life. In fact, block your ex so that you cannot stalk her or him even if you want to.

You're dating again and that makes you happy

In the beginning, you might balk at the idea of dating, or might date people just for the sake of dating (going through the motions). This is because in the back of your mind, you believe your ex is impossible to be replaced and you hold on to that feeling. But don't forget that there are plenty of other fishes in the sea, and those fishes are very capable of keeping you happy as well.

You're okay that your ex moved on

Let's face it. Both of you have to move on – it's just a question of when. But to see your ex move on before you while you're still mending your broken heart can be quite hurtful or angering (depending on your nature). But if you're over them, you don't care what's happening in their lives. You don't have to be happy he moved on, but you have to at least feel nothing or so bad about it.

Bumping into him/her isn't awkward

This is one of the best ways on how to know you've moved on. You don't have to hide here and there in fear of bumping into your ex. That's because you're over that past and now, your ex is just another person in your life whom you don't love. This makes the face to face meeting a lot less awkward.

You don't feel the need to drunk dial her/him

When people are drunk, most of their repressed emotions rise to the surface. They lose their inhibitions, lower their guard and do things they normally wouldn't do. But when you're drunk and you don't feel the need to call him or her, you should know you've truly moved on.

You forget important details about him/her

His or her birthday, first salary, parents' anniversary – these used to be big deal for you and you used to prepare weeks in advance to celebrate such important moments, remember? But now, these days come and go, and most of the times you don't even realize those dates have passed. This is how to know you've moved on.

Remember to keep an open mind towards accepting and healing from emotional stress and heartbreak.

You're loved and you will definitely be OKAY.